Songs
for
Little Cowpokes

Compiled by Ron Middlebrook

 CD recording - arranged, played and produced by Randy Ames

Cover art - Eddie Young
Cover make up - Shawn Brown
Layout - Kenny Warfield
Music notation - Randy Ames
Coloring pages from "Cowboys of the Old West" courtesy of Dover Publications

ISBN 1-57424-201-6
SAN 683-8022

Copyright © 2006 CENTERSTREAM Publishing LLC
P.O. Box 17878 - Anaheim Hills, CA 92817

Table of Contents

Play-A-Long CD Notes:
Each song is played three times. The first and third time with the melody. The second time is played without the melody or the melody is an octave lower so you can sing or play the lead part of the song. Have fun; I hope you enjoy playing and singing these wonderful classic cowboy songs.

The Big Corral 3
Buffalo Gals 4
Colorado Trail 5
A Cow Pony Friend (Old Blue) 6
Doney Gal 8
Green Grow the Lilacs 10
Home on the Range 12
Little Joe the Wrangler 14
Night Herding Song 15
The Old Chisholm Trail 16
Old Paint 17
Ragtime Cowboy Joe 18
The Railroad Corral 20
Red River Shore 22
Red River Valley 24
Red Wing 26
Whoopee Ti-Yi Yo, Git Along Little Dogies 28
The Yellow Rose of Texas 30

Bob   Patsy   Bill   Don

Known as the Patsy (Montana) and the Beeman Bros when they were in the W.L.S. National Barn Dance show at the 1938 Pan American Exposition Worlds Fair held in Dallas, Texas.

The Big Corral

Arizona cowboy and entertainer Romaine Lowdermilk wrote this song in 1922.
The song pokes fun at the camp cook and was based on an English gospel tune.

2. Early in the morning 'bout half-past four,
Press along to the Big Corral.
You'll hear him open his face to roar,
Press along to the big Corral.

3. The wrangler's out a-combing the hills,
Press along to the Big Corral.
So jump in your britches and grease up your gills,
Press along to the Big Corral.

4. The chuck we get ain't fit to eat,
Press along to the Big Corral.
There's rocks in the beans and sand in the meat,
Press along to the Big Corral.

This Arrangement © 2006 by Centerstream Publishing LLC

Buffalo Gals

This old song goes way back, back before the cowboy days with easy to remember words and melody it is well liked by everyone.

2. I asked her if she'd stop and talk, stop and talk, stop and talk,
Her feet covered up the whole sidewalk,
She was fair to view.

3. I asked her if she'd be my wife, be my wife, be my wife,
Then I'd be happy all my life,
If she'd marry me.

Colorado Trail

The Colorado Trail left the trunk line of the Western Trail in Southern Oklahoma and angled off to the northwest through the Texas Panhandle and into Colorado. In Colorado the trail crossed Two Butte Creek and the Purgatorie River ending in La Junta. Long trail driving days and the feelings of a lovesick cowboy are both here in this herding song.

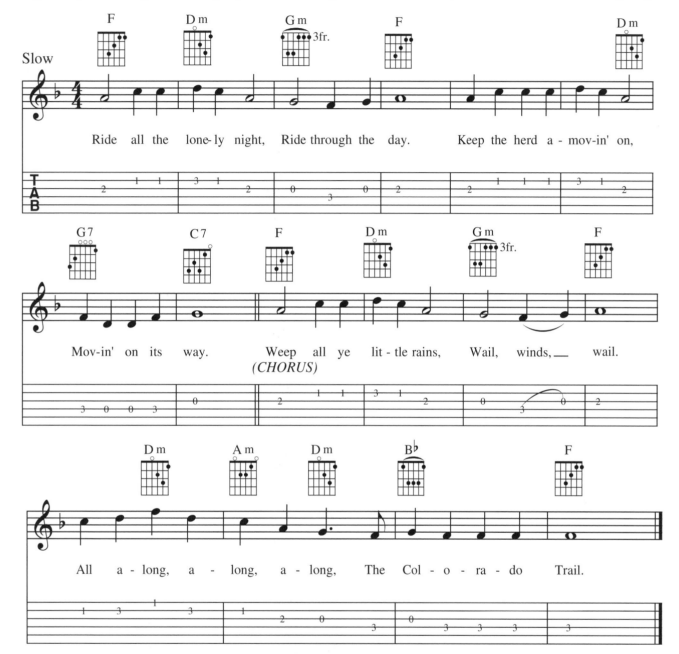

Ride all the lone-ly night, Ride through the day. Keep the herd a - mov-in' on,

Mov-in' on its way. Weep all ye lit - tle rains, Wail, winds, __ wail.
(CHORUS)

All a - long, a - long, a - long, The Col - o - ra - do Trail.

2. Eyes like the morning star,
   Cheeks like a rose.
   Laura was a pretty girl,
   God Almighty knows.

Chorus

3. Ride through the stormy night,
   Dark is the sky.
   Wish I'd stayed in Abilene,
   Nice and warm and dry.

Chorus

The Edison family

A Cow Pony Friend

(Old Blue)

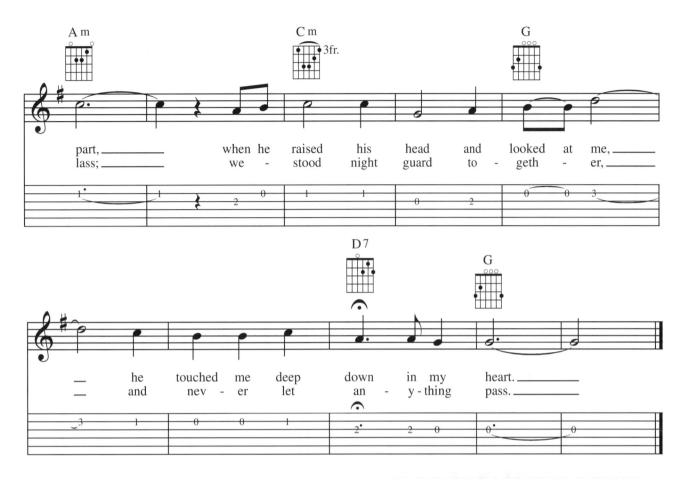

part, _____ when he raised his head and looked at me, _____
lass; _____ we - stood night guard to - geth - er, _____

he touched me deep down in my heart. _____
and nev - er let an - y - thing pass. _____

3. Then you stabled me and fed me next winter;
   Taught me how to hold a steer down.
   I'd sit back on the rope 'till it almost broke,
   But I'd never let one off the ground.
   Your praise was just like music;
   You never a cross word spoke,
   When we lost the rope contest at Dixon,
   And I knew old friend, you were broke.

4. And then you got into trouble,
   And went on the dodge for a time,
   And the ride that we made for the river,
   And midnight crossed the line.
   Eighty miles on the sand without water,
   In the heat of an August day,
   'Till we ran the legs off the posse,
   Crossed the border and got away.

5. When the years passed you gave me my freedom,
   Wouldn't let me die in a pen,
   But turned me loose on the green hills
   That I might recover again.
   Good-bye, Master, I'll ask a last favor:
   Be as good as you've been to me
   To the rest of your mount of cow horses;
   When worn out and old, turn them free.

The Lone Ranger.

7

Doney Gal

A night herding song and one of the best about a cowboy's horse. Doney Gal meant sweetheart.
Often the name of a favorite girl was used for a favorite horse, I wonder how the girls felt about that?
Play this one slow. Alan Lomax believes that it is one of the last of the genuine cowboy songs.

Prelude:
We're alone, Doney Gal, in the wind and hail.
Gotta drive these dogies down the trail.

Chorus:
It's rain or shine, sleet or snow,
Me and my Doney Gal are bound to go.
Yes, rain or shine, sleet or snow,
Me and my Doney Gal are on the go.
A cowboy's life is a dreary thing,
For it's rope, and brand, and ride and sing.
Yes, day or night in rain or hail,
We'll stay with the doggies on the trail.

3.   We travel down that lonesome trail,
      Where a man and his horse seldom ever fail.
      We laugh at storms, sleet and snow,
      When we camp near San Antonio.

4.   Tired and hungry, far from home,
      I'm just a poor cowboy and bound to roam.
      Starless nights and lightning glare,
      Danger and darkness everywhere.

5.   Drifting my Doney Gal round and round,
      Steers are asleep on a new bed ground.
      Riding night herd all night long,
      Singing softly a cowboy song.

6.   Swimming rivers along the way,
      Pushing for the North Star day by day.
      Storm clouds break, and at breakneck speed,
      We follow the steers in a wild stampede.

7.   Over the prairies lean and brown
      And on through wastes where there ain't no town.
      Bucking dust storms, wind and hail,
      Pushing the longhorns up the trail.

8.   Trailing the herd through mountains green,
      We pen all the cattle at Abilene.
      Then round the campfire's flickering glow
      We sing the songs of long ago.

Green Grow the Lilacs

An old Irish song, widely popular with the early Texas Cowboys. A colorful fable holds that the Mexican word "gringo" meaning cowboy, was derived from the song, for the Mexicans referred to the Americans by the first two words of the title "Green Grow," pronouncing it "Gringo". True or not, it makes a good story.

2. I used to have a sweetheart, but now I have none,
   Since she's gone and left me, I care not for one.
   Since she's gone and left me, contented I'll be,
   For she loves another one better than me.

3. I passed my love's window, both early and late,
   The look that she gave me, it made my heart ache.
   Oh, the look that she gave me was painful to see,
   For she loves another one better than me.

4. I wrote my love letters in rosy red lines,
   She sent me an answer all twisted in twines,
   Saying, 'Keep your love letters and I will keep mine,
   Just you write to your love and I'll write to mine.'

5. Green grow the lilacs, all sparking with dew,
   I'm lonely, my darling, since parting with you,
   But by our next meeting I'll hope to prove true,
   And change the green lilacs to Red, White and Blue.

William Frederick Cody (Buffalo Bill) was a frontier scout, pony express rider, buffalo hunter, army guide, Indian fighter, wild west showman, and hero of Ned Buntline dime novels.

Charles Goodnight was a Texas Ranger, Indian fighter and Pioneer cattle rancher. Both the Goodnight Trail and Goodnight-Loving Trail are named for him. First bred the "cattalo."

Phoebe Anne Oakley Mozee (Annie Oakley) was nicknamed "little Sure Shot," she was a major star of Buffalo Bill Cody's Wild West Show for seventeen years.

Willie M. Pickett (Bill Pickett) was a fearless black cowboy, rodeo showman and rancher, said to have invented bulldogging. Both Will Rogers and Tom Mix served as his assistants.

Home on the Range

Oscar J. Fox, San Antonio, Texas, published an arrangement of this song after it had remained unnoticed for many years in *Cowboy Songs*. For a time "Home on the Range" was the most popular song on the air.

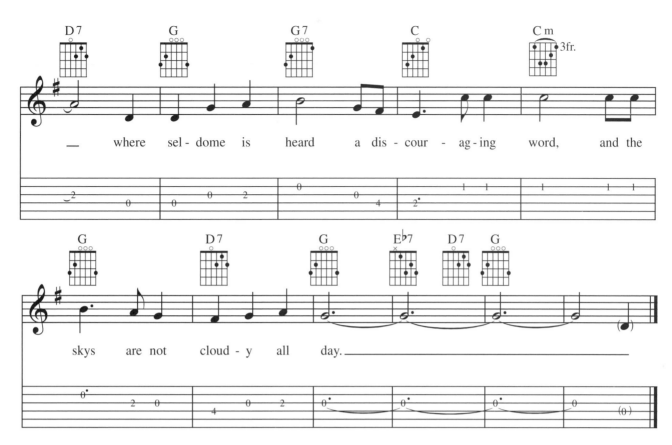

where sel - dome is heard a dis - cour - ag - ing word, and the

skys are not cloud - y all day. _____

Where the air is so pure, the
Zephyers so free,
The breezes so balmy and light,
That I would not exchange my
home on the range
For all the cities so bright.

The red man was pressed from
his part of the West,
He's likely no more to return
To the banks of Red River
where seldom if ever
Their flickering campfires burn.

Dylan

Little Joe the Wrangler

This song about Little Joe is from an actual happening on the trail. It was written by pioneer collector of cowboy songs, Nathan Howard "Jack" Thorp. In 1898 Jack Thorp helped trail a herd of O cattle from Chimney Lake, New Mexico, to Higgins, Texas. One night while sitting by the campfire, Jack took an old paper bag and a stub of a pencil and wrote the song of Little Joe, a wrangler he once knew. He sang it to the tune of "Little Old Log Cabin in the Lane."

2. It was long late in the evening when he rode up to our herd,
On an old brown pony he called Chaw.
With his brogan shoes and overalls, a harder looking kid
You never in your life had seen before.

3. His saddle was a Southern kack built many years ago,
An O.K. spur on one foot idly hung.
His hot roll in a cotton sack was loosely tied behind,
And a canteen from his saddle horn he'd slung.

This Arrangement © 2006 by Centerstream Publishing LLC

Night Herding Song

Range cattle on a strange bed-ground are as nervous as a cat in a room full of rocking chairs. They sniff and pace and mill, and any sudden noise may set off a stampede. The night herding cowboys on duty keep up a constant clucking, whistling, crooning and singing to the rhythm of their walking horse, to quiet the cattle, as well as to keep themselves from dozing in the saddle. This song appealing to those restless little dogies is one of the more beautiful ones.

2. I've circle-herded, trail-herded, night-herded too.
    But to keep you all together is all I can do.
    My horse is leg-weary and I'm awful tired,
    If you get away, I will be fired -
    Buch up, little dogies, buch up

3. O, say little dogies, when you gonna lay down,
    And quit this forever a-shifting around?
    My limbs are weary and my seat is all sore,
    Lay down like you've laid down before -
    Lay down, little dogies, lay down.

The Old Chisholm Trail

If ever a song could be called a cowbow song it is this one. Jesse Chisholm was a real man, an Indian trader and interpreter, who in 1866, found a route over which to drive Texas longhornes from San Antonio to the nearest railroad at Abeline, Kansas, a distance of 800 miles. It is said to have a stanza for every mile along the way.

Oh come a-long boys, and lis-ten to my tale, I'll

tell you all my troub-les on the Ol' 'Chis' m trail. Come a - ti - yi - you-py you-py
(CHORUS)

ya you-py yay, Come a - ti - yi - you-py you-py yay.

On a ten-dollar horse and a forty-dollar saddle,
I was ridin', and a-punchin' Texas cattle.

I woke up one mornin' on the Chisholm trail,
With a rope in my hand and a cow by the tail.

Oh the wind commenced to blow and the rain began to fall,
An' it looked by grab that we was gonna lose 'em all.

I jumped in the saddle an' I grabbed a-holt the horn,
The best darn cowpuncher ever was born.

I was on my best horse, and a-goin' on the run,
The quickest-shootin' cowboy that ever pulled a gun.

No chaps, no slicker, and it's pourin' down rain,
An' I swear, by God, I'll never night herd again.

I herded and I hollered, and I done pretty well
Till the boss said, "Boy's, just let them go to Heck."

I went to the boss to draw my roll,
He figgered me out nine dollars in the hole.

So I'll sell my outfit as fast as I can,
And I won't punch cows for no darn man.

So I sold old Baldy and I hung up my saddle,
And I bid farewell to the longhorn cattle.

Jesse Chisholm

Old Paint

One of the great night-herding songs. "Old Paint" like "Chisholm Trail" is a formula song: improvisation is easy, each singer uses his one selection of couplets. The rhythm is slow and meditative.

I'm rid - ing Old Paint, I'm lead - ing Old Dan, I'm off for Chey -

enne ___ to do the hool - o - han. My foot's in the stir - rup, my

po - ny won't ___ stand; Good - bye, Old Paint, ___ I'm leav - ing Chey -

enne, Good - bye, Old Paint, ___ I'm leav - ing Chey - enne.

Ragtime Cowboy Joe

mu-sic to the cat-tle, as he swings back and for-ward in the sad-dle on a horse that is

syn -co-pat-ed, gait-ed. And there's such a fun-ny met-er to the roar of his re-peat-er, how they run when they

hear the fel-low's gun, be-cause the west-ern folks all know, he's a high fa-lu-ting, scoot-ing shoot-ing

son-of-a-gun from Ar - i - zo - na, Rag-time, Cow-boy Joe.___ He al - ways Joe.

The Railroad Corral

Happy cowboys getting the steers from range to train, this rousing song was written in
1904 by Joseph Hanson. It was included in the first Lomax collection in 1910.

ral. *(INSTRUMENTAL)*

Oh we're up in the morn-ing ere break-ing of day, the ___
(VERSE)

chuck wag-on's bus-y the flap-jack's in play; the herd is a-stir ___ o'er

hill-side and vale, with the night ri-ders round-ing them in-to the trail.
(To Chorus)

2. Oh, come take up your cinches, come shake out your reins;
Come wake your old broncos and break for the plains;
come roust out your steers from the long chaparral,
For the outfit is off to the railroad corral.

To Refrain

3. The sun circles upward; the steers as they plod
Are pounding to powder the hot prairie sod;
Now it seems as the dust makes you dizzy and sick
That we'll never reach noon and the cool, shady creek

To Refrain

4. Now tie up your kerchief and ply up your nag,
Come dry up your grumbles and try not to lag;
Come with you steers from the long chaparral,
For we're far on the road to the railroad corral.

To Refrain

Red River Shore

A narrative song, " I met a fair maiden, the girl I adore," who lives beneath a mountain on the Red River Shore. Her father refuses her hand to the cowboy, who jumps on his bronco and rides away. But the sorrowing girl summons him back with a letter. By the time he reaches the Red River Shore, however, she had drowned herself in despair.

3. I asked her old father, if he'd give her to me.
    "No sir, she shan't marry no cowboy," said he.
    So I jumped on my bronco and away I did ride
    A-leaving my true love on the Red River side.

4. Her cruel old father did thus interfere,
    Saying he would deprive her of the dearest so dear;
    He would send him away where the cannon do roar
    Away from his true love on the Red River shore.

5. She wrote me a letter, and she wrote it so kind,
    And in this letter these words you could find;
    "Come back to me darling; you're the one I adore,
    You're the one I would marry on the Red River shore.

6. I read this letter through till it made my heart sad,
    And none of the fellows could make my heart glad;
    Now I'm not used to stoppin', and you may be sure
    I was bound for my true love on the Red River shore.

7. So I jumped on my bronco and away I did ride
    To marry my true love on the Red River side.
    But her dad knew the secret, and with twenty and four
    Came to fight this young cowboy on the Red River shore.

8. I drew my six-shooter, spun around and around
    Till six men were wounded and seven were down.
    No use for an army of twenty and four;
    I'm bound for my true love on the Red River shore.

9. Such is the fortune of all womenkind,
    They are always controlled, they are always made mind;
    Controlled by their parents until they become wives,
    And slaves of their husbands the rest of their lives.

10. Hard luck in this world for all womenkind;
    To those who are single the world o'er I find –
    Confined with their parent's until they are wives,
    And stay with their husbands the rest of their lives.

Trevor

Red River Valley

Originally a Canadian love song, with the Red River of the North as its setting, it became a cowboy song about the Red River of the Texas-Oklahoma cattle country and it gained widespread appeal to finally become one of the favorite folk songs of America.

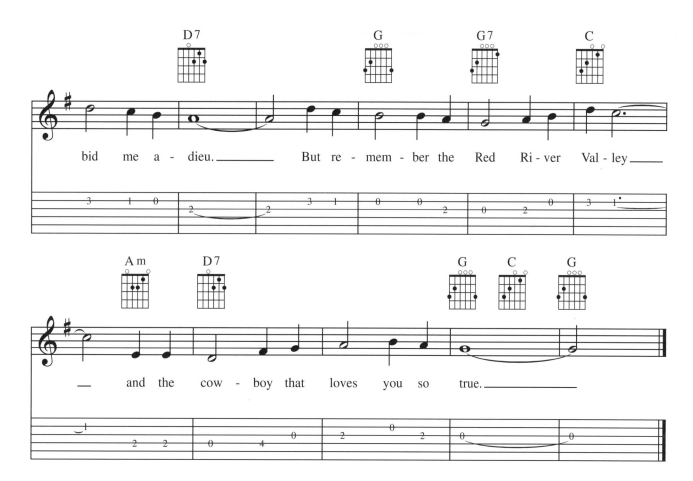

bid   me   a - dieu._____   But   re - mem - ber   the   Red   Ri - ver   Val - ley_____

_____   and   the   cow - boy   that   loves   you   so   true._____

2. From this valley they say you are going,
   I will miss your sweet face and your smile.
   Just because you are weary and tired,
   You are changing your range for awhile.

3. I've been waiting a long time my darling,
   For the sweet words you never would say.
   Now at last all my fond hopes have vanished,
   For they say you are going away.

4. O there never could be such a longing
   In the heart of a poor cowboy's breast.
   That now dwells in the heart you are breaking,
   As I wait in my home in the West.

5. Do you think of the valley you're leaving?
   O how lonely and drear it will be!
   Do you think of the kind heart you're breaking,
   And the pain you are causing to me?

6. As you go to your home by the ocean,
   May you never forget those sweet hours
   That we spent in the Red River Valley,
   And the love we exchanged mid the flowers.

The Chance brothers, Slim and None.

Red Wing

Published in 1907, this song was composed by Mills and Chattway. Mills' music is based on a 1849 piece by Schumann. Many songs were written about romantizied Indians in the early 1900's. Red Wing became the most popular and the most parodied.

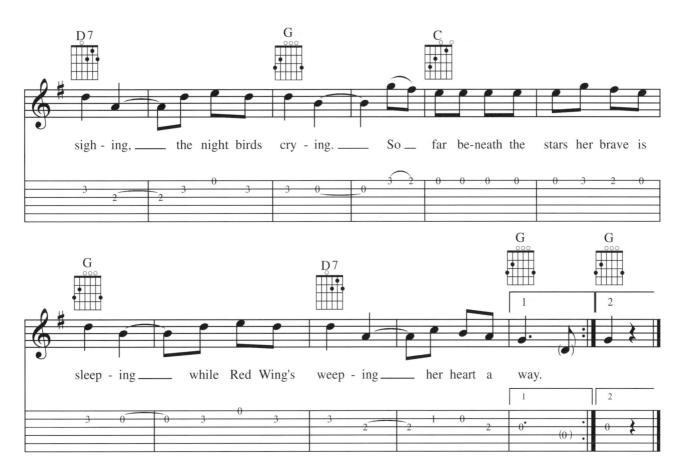

sigh - ing, _____ the night birds cry - ing. _____ So _ far be-neath the stars her brave is

sleep - ing _____ while Red Wing's weep - ing _____ her heart a way.

Ethan

Whoopee Ti-Yi Yo, Git Along Little Dogies

This trail song was first published in 1910 by John Lomax. He first heard it sung by a Gypsy woman who was camped in a grove of trees near the cattle pens of the Fort Worth, Texas, Stockyards.

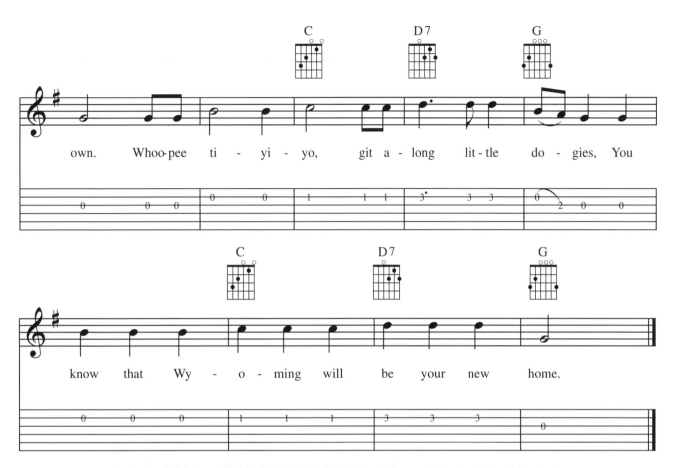

own. Whoo-pee ti - yi - yo, git a - long lit - tle do - gies, You

know that Wy - o - ming will be your new home.

Cowgirls: Ber Kirnan, Prairie Rose, Mable Strickland, Princis Mohawk, Ruth Roach, Kittie Canutt and Prairie Little.

2. Early in the springtime we round up the dogies,
   Mark 'em, and brand 'em and bob off their tail;
   Round up the horses, load up the chuck wagon,
   Then throw the little dogies out on the long trail.

3. Night comes on and we hold 'em on the bed ground.
   The same little dogies that rolled on so slow.
   We roll up the herd and cut out the stray ones,
   Then roll the little dogies like never before.

4. Some boys go up the long trail for pleasure,
   But that's where they get it most awfully wrong.

For you'll never know the trouble they give us
As we go driving the dogies along.

5. Your mother was raised away down in Texas,
   Where the jimson weeds and sandburs grow.
   We'll fill you up on prickly pear and cholla,
   Then throw you on the trail to Idaho.

6. O, you'll be soup for Uncle Sam's Injuns.
   Git along, git along, git along little dogies;
   It's "Beef, heap beef!" I hear them cry.
   You'll all be beef steers in the sweet by-and-by.

The Yellow Rose of Texas

Although the song did not originate with the cowboys, it was popular with them. "The Yellow Rose of Teaxas" was issued on sheet music form in 1858.

There's a yel-low rose in Tex-as I'm go-in there to see. No

oth-er cow-boy knows her, no - bod-y on - ly me. She cried so when I

left her, it liked to broke her heart, and if we ev - er meet a - gain we

nev-er more shall part. She's the sweet-est rose of col - or this
(CHORUS)

cow-boy ev - er knew. Her eyes are bright as dia-monds, they spar-kel like the

dew. You may talk a-bout your dear-est maids and sing of Ro-sy Lee, but the

yel-low rose of Tex - as beats the belles of Ten - nes - see.

2. Where the Rio Grande is flowing and the stars are shining bright,
   We walked along together on a quiet summer night.
   She said, " If you remember we parted long ago.
   You promised to come back again and never leave me so."

3. O, I'm going back to see her, my heart is full of woe.
   We'll sing the songs together we sang so long ago.
   I'll pick the banjo gaily and sing the songs of yore,
   And the yellow rose of Texas will be mine forevermore.

**Jerry Poolaw,
Mountain View,
Oklahoma, 1929.**

31

Color this page.

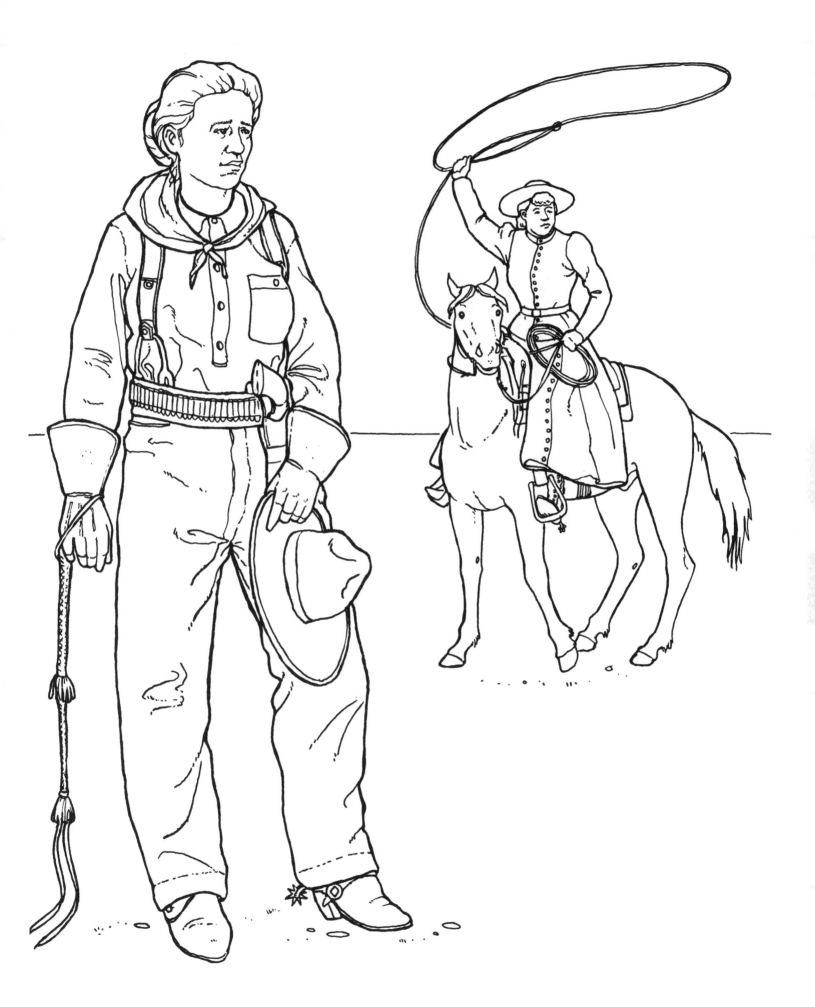

Color this page.

Color this page.

Color this page.